Balancing Bears: Comparing Numbers

by Megan Atwood

illustrated by Sharon Holm

Content Consultant: Paula J. Maida, PhD

magic wagon

VISIT US AT
WWW.ABDOPUBLISHING.COM

Published by Magic Wagon, a division of the ABDO Group, PO Box 398166, Minneapolis, MN 55439. Copyright © 2012 by Abdo Consulting Group, Inc. International copyrights reserved in all countries. All rights reserved. No part of this book may be reproduced in any form without written permission from the publisher.

Looking Glass Library™ is a trademark and logo of Magic Wagon.

Printed in the United States of America, North Mankato, Minnesota.
102011
012012

Text by Megan Atwood
Illustrations by Sharon Holm
Edited by Lisa Owings
Interior layout by Kazuko Collins
Cover design by Christa Schneider

Library of Congress Cataloging-in-Publication Data

Atwood, Megan.
  Balancing bears : comparing numbers / by Megan Atwood ; illustrated by Sharon Lane Holm.
    p. cm. — (Count the critters)
  ISBN 978-1-61641-851-9
  1. Number concept — Juvenile literature. I. Holm, Sharon Lane, ill. II. Title.
  QA141.3.A89 2012
  512.7 — dc23
                        2011033073

Comparing numbers is fun! These bears like to balance berries on their paws and noses. You can use symbols to compare numbers of berries.

The symbol for less than is this: <.
The symbol for greater than is this: >.
The symbol for equal to is this: =.

Bears rustle and wrestle. Bears are omnivores. They eat meat and plants and berries. Two bear cubs rustle in the bushes for berries. One picks three berries. He balances them on his nose. The other bear cub has four berries. Which number is smaller? Three is less than four.

Bears wrestle and rustle. Two sister bears wrestle near their brothers. One stands up with four berries in her paws. The other stands up with six berries. Which number is smaller? Four is less than six.

7   8   9   10   4 < 6

Bears share and sniff. One sister bear shares berries with her brother. Brother bear has eight berries. Sister bear has three berries. Which number is bigger? Eight is greater than three.

7　　8　　9　　10　　8 > 3

Bears sniff and share. A bear's sense of smell is its most powerful sense. Sister bear sniffs out more tasty berries. Now she has four berries. Her brother has two berries. Which number is bigger? Four is greater than two.

7   8   9   10   4 > 2

Bears balance and bounce. Bears can balance on their hind legs. This helps them see better. One brother bear stands on his hind legs. He balances seven berries on his nose. Sister bear also balances seven berries. The numbers are the same! Seven is equal to seven.

Bears bounce and balance. One sister bear balances eight berries on her nose. She shows off by bouncing them!

1 2 3 4 5 6

Brother bear can bounce eight berries, too. The numbers are the same! Eight is equal to eight.

7 8 9 10 8 = 8

Bears clap and cuddle. Mama bear balances ten berries on her nose. She can balance two more than her cubs.

1   2   3   4   5   6

The bear cubs clap for their mama.

Eight is less than ten.

7   8   9   10   8 < 10

1 2 3 4 5 6

Bears cuddle and clap. Mama bears are very protective of their cubs. Mama bear wraps her arms around her cubs. The bear cubs cuddle their mama. Mama bear gives her cubs eight berries. She keeps two for herself. Eight is greater than two.

Bears rustle and wrestle, share and sniff, balance and bounce, and clap and cuddle. Bears are always hungry! They must eat all the berries they can find before winter comes. Mama bear makes sure all her cubs get equal numbers of berries.

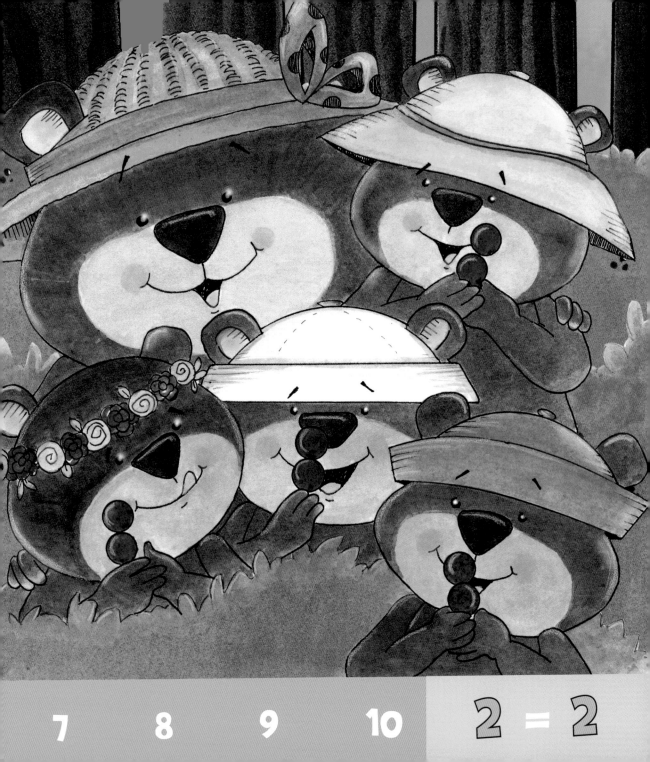

7 8 9 10 2 = 2

Now you can compare numbers!

< less than

> greater than

= equal to

2 = 2

Bears love berries!

3 > 2   2 < 3

Words to Know

bounce — to hit a surface and spring back up.

cuddle — to hold close.

omnivore — an animal that eats both meat and plants.

protective — having a strong wish to keep something safe.

rustle — to look for food.

symbol — an image that stands for a word.

wrestle — a contest where two individuals struggle to unbalance each other.

Web Sites

To learn more about comparing numbers, visit ABDO Group online at **www.abdopublishing.com**. Web sites about comparing numbers are featured on our Book Links page. These links are routinely monitored and updated to provide the most current information available.

< less than   > greater than   = equal to